C000017134

JUST

Just a Moment, Lord, the first book of prayer poems by Flora
Larsson, was published in 1973. It was followed by *Between You
and Me, Lord*; *Towards You, Lord*; *God in my Everyday* and *My
God and I*.

This Classic Salvationist Texts edition of *Just a Moment, Lord* is
a revised and updated version of the original book. A few prayer
poems have been replaced with others drawn from the four
other books in order to recognise the treasury these represent.
Full details of sources can be found at the end of this book.

JUST A MOMENT, LORD

by

Flora Larsson

Salvation Books
The Salvation Army International Headquarters
London, United Kingdom

First published in 1973 by Hodder and Stoughton
ISBN 0 340 17668 7
Reissued in 1984 by Marshall Morgan & Scott
ISBN 0 551 01123 8

This revised and expanded edition published 2012

Copyright © 2012
The General of The Salvation Army

ISBN 978-0-85412-862-4
e-book ISBN 978-0-85412-863-1

Project editors Majors Trevor Howes and David Dalziel
and Paul Mortlock
Cover design by Berni Georges

Published by Salvation Books
The Salvation Army International Headquarters
101 Queen Victoria Street, London EC4V 4EH
United Kingdom

Printed in the UK by Page Bros., Norwich

SERIES INTRODUCTION
'CLASSIC SALVATIONIST TEXTS'

THE Bible often underscores the importance of speaking into the next generation. It is for this reason that Salvation Army 'classics' are being republished. A new generation of readers needs to and wants to hear from our godly Salvationists from the past who lived out their faith and wrote about it with conviction and humility. What a heritage we have and these writings share something of the richness of it!

The psalmist David declares, 'One generation will commend your works to another; they will tell of your mighty acts. They will speak of the glorious splendour of your majesty' (Psalm 145:4-5 *NIV*). In the verses that follow he continues to explain what those of one generation will say to the next when they pass on the faith.

May the Lord draw us even closer to him as we hear with our hearts what he has spoken through his Salvationist servants. And may we be challenged not only to learn from them but also to leave a legacy ourselves in our time, through our living and our communication of the deep things of God.

Linda Bond
General
London, November 2012

CONTENTS

LEARNING IN GOD'S SCHOOL

UNKNOWN TOMORROWS

GOOD DAYS AND BAD

My heart sings

Today my heart sings, Lord;
Everything within me rejoices.

> Joy bubbles up in my soul,
> overflows and cascades like a stream leaping
>   all barriers;
> the joy of knowing you,
> the joy of union with you.

One with you, Creator of the world,
    and my Creator,
One with you, Saviour of the world,
    and my Saviour.
One with you, Spirit of the eternal God,
    and my God,
One with you, almighty King of kings
    and my Lord and King.

> Joy, joy at the heart of living,
> joy in doing, joy in being;
> sing for joy, my heart,
> for sheer joy, my soul.

> The joy of loving you,
> the joy of following you,

the joy of serving you;
all the way 'long it is glory.

Today my heart sings, Lord;
everything within me rejoices,
joy bubbles up in my soul,
glory … glory!

Where are you?

Master, where are you?
Yesterday I knew.
> Yesterday I rejoiced in your love;
> Your presence enhanced each task;
> Your comfort filled my heart.

Today, where are you?
> Withdrawn?
> Why, Lord?

Today is empty.
> Today has no joys;
> today has no wings;
> today has no glad future;
All is drear, meaningless.
> Why, Lord?

Has the veil of my flesh thickened so as to shut you
out?
Have the shutters of my mind snapped together?

Have I carelessly left the blinds drawn on the
windows of my soul?

Show me, Master, if the fault is mine.
Help me to put it right,
and, if it is simply a weakness of the earthen vessel
that bears your likeness without your
power,
help me still to believe in you;
to hold on in trust until my soul revives.

For I'm lonely without you, Lord,
and without you I cannot live.

Courage to live

Lord, give me courage to live!
A cheerful courage, Master, if that might be.
Let me wear a smile even when my heart trembles;
let laughter-lines form round my eyes,
and let me hold my chin up
and go forward.

Lord, give me courage to live!
A grim, unsmiling courage, if need be.
Courage to face the empty days,
unfulfilled hopes,
black hours,
defeats, maybe;
A hard, defiant courage, that will hang on

until things are better.
Grant me that, Lord.

Master, give me courage to live!
One of your servants wrote that 'in the dark,
        brave souls hold on to the skirts of God'.
Give me courage like that, Lord,
        clinging courage, desperate courage,
        that will not let you go.
If feeling goes, if faith goes, if fortitude fails,
        let me just hold on,
        clinging to you,
        knowing that you are there,
        counting on you to see me through.

An awful day

Today, Lord, has been awful!
        It started badly.
Imps of depression sat on the bedposts
        waiting for me to wake,
        ready to pounce on me,
        to harry me
        and fill me with their gloom.

My head ached, my nerves were edgy
        and I felt irritable.

And then it rained …
not a decent sort of rain, soon over and done with,

but a penetrating, miserable, drooling kind of rain
that wet-blanketed soul as well as body.

There are days like that, Master.
Days when life is heavy, boring, meaningless;
days when no ray pierces the inward gloom,
        just plain bad days.

What is your recipe for such hours, Lord?
I am reminded of some words which were often on
            your lips,
        'Take heart!'
They must have comforted your followers many
            times.
You used them when they were startled,
        when they had lost their nerve,
        when they needed encouragement.

I need encouragement, Master,
so I quieten my mind and wait to hear you say,
        'Take heart!'
Thank you, Lord.

My mind races

I can't be still, Lord, as you command.
        My body is immobile,
        but my mind races;
        leaps from one subject to another;
        flies off at a tangent.

In the distance I hear the soft chiming of a church clock.
Outside my window seagulls ride on the wind,
the friendly sparrows enjoy a morning chat.
A neighbour waters her flowers.

And yet my mind races on though my body
          remains relaxed.
      The past, the present, the future.
      What I have done,
      should have done,
      still have to do.

Things press upon my mind from all directions.
      I feel chased,
      burdened,
      overwhelmed.

How do I find your peace, Lord?
      Peace within me,
      a quiet mind,
      a tranquil heart.
These are what I need,
and these are what you have promised.

      Make me receptive, Master.
      Let me feel your peace flowing into my
         mind,
      stilling the inward storms,
      calming and quieting,
      soothing and strengthening.
      Just now, Lord, now.

A perfect day

I want to thank you for a perfect day, Lord.
Everything has gone right,
every single little thing, as well as the big things.
There was sunshine this morning, with tiny white
clouds sailing across the blue heavens,
the dewy flowers laughed at me as I walked down
the garden path,
and roses wafted their delicious scent in my
direction.

Heavenly Father, when you planned your world,
why did you make it so breathtakingly
beautiful?
It hurts, Lord,
so much beauty hurts.
It makes a pain inside that is a pain of joy,
a quivering, glowing, lovely little pain
that bursts into the heart and fills it.

I hardly dare to live in your world when you show
its splendours.
It is too big for me,
too marvellous.
But into the small world of my home I fit.
There I can be myself, and the hours alone are not
hours of loneliness,
except at times.

Today, though, joy has filled my heart.
African violets nodded to me from the window sill,

and the radio played such happy tunes that I
        danced across the floor as I dusted,
which resulted in very skimpy dusting, Lord.
But you understand, don't you?

I was too happy to bother about such trifles as
        specks of dust,
        so thank you.
Thank you a thousand times for this happy day.
        Good night.

Mist on the hills

Mist on the hills!
Fog on the roads,
the outlook gloomy with a sense of unreality.
An uncomfortable feeling of being choked,
enclosed by a stifling grey blanket.

Teach me to live on my memories, Lord.
        To picture the distant mountain,
        the sunlight glinting on the river,
        patterned by the wake of small boats.

The unseen is there, is real and living!
Let me rejoice in that knowledge and await;
        clarity of vision will return.

So too, Lord, let it be in my spiritual life.
When clouds imprison me
and faith is dulled;
when love is cold
and truth seems dead.

Then let me call to mind your former graciousness.
Moments when my heart responded,
when my soul rejoiced in your presence,
my faith shone bright and firm.

The unseen is there, is real and living!
Let me rejoice in that knowledge and await;
clarity of vision will return.

Yesterday

Yesterday is an old garment, Lord,
creased, stained and threadbare.
Help me to throw it off,
casting it into the coffers of the past,
done with, laid aside and forgotten.

Let me not walk in my yesterdays;
not live again the used-up hours,
regretting the misspent moments,
brooding over the rebuffs,
fingering the tattered glory-rags,
clutching them close to my eager breast.

Today is new, fresh from your hands,
     glowing with promise of fulfilment,
     full of opportunities,
     of duties,
     of joys;
     with perhaps a tinge of sorrow.

Let me wear 'today' hopefully,
     grateful that it is mine,
     glad to face its challenge,
     using unstintingly
     each moment as it comes.

For tonight, Master, tonight I must lay it off,
     an old garment,
     creased, stained and threadbare,
     casting it into the coffers of the past,
     done with, laid aside and forgotten.

Courage for today

Lord, give me courage for today!
I dare not look ahead into the vista
     of far-stretching time
     or tomorrow's tasks,
but for one day, this single day,
     grant me courage, Lord.
Courage to tackle the duties to be done,
courage to face the people I must meet,
courage to hold my head high though I quail.
     Grant me quiet courage, Lord.

Let me show a brave face despite inward desolation,
      the sudden panic of aloneness,
      fears for the future,
or simply a nameless dread that grips me
      with cold clammy hands.
Grant me courage for today, Master.

Just for this day, Lord, grant me sustaining grace,
      strength for each hour that comes,
      valour when my heart feels faint;
may I sound plucky when my nerve fails.
Let me reach the evening hours having won through,
      perhaps not gloriously,
      yet adequately.
Let the thin thread of my endurance stretch
      to its utmost limits,
because it is strengthened and sustained by you.

For this one day, Lord, I pray.
      Help me through it,
and when night comes I shall thank you
      from a grateful heart.

Tides

There is ebb and flow in spiritual tides, Lord,
for we are not always at our best.
There is despair in the ebb
when the sand wastes are revealed
      and rocks loom dangerously near.

Fears suck courage away
as a weight of loneliness crushes the soul
        and prayers die on the lips.

But there comes the turn of the tide,
        a flicker of hope,
        a clutch at faith,
        a whispered prayer.
The creeping waves of the incoming spiritual tide
        fill up the empty creek
        with movement, sound and hope.
Then once again comes the full flood of the Spirit,
the soul soars in vibrant faith, words of praise
        pouring from the mouth
        and joy filling the heart.

Must it be so, Master?
        Ebb and flood,
        much and little,
        gloom and glory,
        comfort and despair?
Our very humanity creates this rhythm
        but *you are stable*!
Thank you, Lord.

This one day

This one day, Lord, is mine.
Your gift to me, fresh from your hands;
        heralded by the twittering of birds,
        cleansed by the dawn wind,

warmed by the sun's first rays ...
This day is mine!

This one shining day is my own.
I bless its early hours
as I commit it to you.
I yield myself into your care
knowing I am secure in your love,
whatever the coming hours may bring.

Please, Master, make it a good day,
filled with happy work-hours
and rewarding leisure,
a really-good-to-be-alive day.

Let today be a day I shall remember,
not because of some world-shaking event,
but because it was a golden day,
glowing with happiness.

Let it be a day of inward harmony and outward peace,
of joybells within
and laughter without;
a carefree rollicking kind of a day
when my heart spins its own thread of fun,
to weave a bright pattern through all that happens.

And when I lay my head on my pillow tonight,
let my heart be warm with gratitude to you
for all life's good gifts.
Let my last thought be a contented:
'Thank you, Lord.'

THE MOTLEY CROWD

WITHIN

Saint in Embryo

There's a strange fellow lives within me, Master,
      He calls himself 'Saint in Embryo'.
How much saint there is about him, I don't know,
but he sure is embryonic.
Sometimes I hardly know that he exists.
      Saint in Embryo leads a hard life, Lord.
      Everything is against him.
      He always has to row against the tide
      and battle with contrary winds.

He will insist on lugging that over-polished halo
      with him,
      and when he has said something good, really
      good,
      or done something fine, really fine,
      instead of leaving matters there
      and slipping quietly away,
He spoils things by putting on his old halo,
      which sits at a rakish angle,
      being too big for him.

Lord, he makes himself ridiculous.
Why can't he learn to do good stealthily,
to be good without being puffed up with pride?

I've remonstrated with him about that halo,
      Master,
      but he says he is forced to wear it
      or people won't know he's trying to be a saint.

When I pointed out that it didn't matter what
        others thought
        but only what you thought
        he looked a bit ashamed
        and tried to hide his halo behind his back.

This Saint in Embryo has got a lot to learn, Master.
Will you take him in hand and train him?

Big Me

Today, Lord, has been a bad day.
Big Me obscured my vision.
Not only my vision of other people and their
        interests,
        that would have been bad enough,
        but worse, Master.
Big Me obscured my vision of you.

This bloated, arrogant Self took the upper hand,
        and I let him do it;
        not with absolute approval,
        but yet with my consent.

Big Me had had a hard day,
he had been ignored, squashed, belittled …
        Big Me was furious
        and rampant,
        on the warpath.

And, Lord, he blotted you out,
    with his swollen self-importance
    he blurred the outlines of your face.

I sat in a sacred service.
One of your servants was proclaiming the rich
        mercies of your grace;
    I only heard Big Me's complaints.
The congregation sang the triumphs of your love;
    Big Me drowned their praise with his
        raucous voice.
Tender verses from your book were read;
    Big Me was unmoved.

What can I do, Master, when Big Me takes the reins?
Can you deliver me from his dominance?

Self-pity

Lord, there's someone lurking within me:
Shrouded and gloomy she goes her way
    with downcast eyes,
    dragging steps,
    and doleful mien.

She's the shadow of a better me.
She's something good gone sour,
self-replete and self-stifled.

To hear her talk is a revelation;
no one ever had it so bad.

21

Her setbacks are unrivalled,
her problems mountain-high.
Turned in upon herself she mopes and broods,
        sobs and sighs;
            poor me ... poor me ...
            poor miserable me!

Out upon you, traitor, I cry:
I'll have none of your mournful dirges ...
away with you from my house of life!

Master, give me courage to throw her out;
Let me get rid of her once and for all,
and bar the door against her.

Help me to bear bravely my own share of life's burdens.
Help me to find others who also suffer
        and try to bring them comfort.
Let me take another's hand in mine and say:
        Courage! the storm will pass;
        look up, day will soon dawn.

Lord, save me from self-pity.

Touchy

Master, may I introduce Touchy?
I'm not exactly proud of him, I can assure you.
Touchy has lived with me since I was a teenager;
        an unwelcome but most persistent lodger,

who takes upon himself an old lodger's
     privilege
of making himself at home
and trying to rule.

Touchy has invisible tentacles that stick out in all
          directions,
with the inevitable result that he's always getting hurt:
     hurt in feelings,
     hurt in his affections,
     hurt in his self-esteem.

He takes offence at the most innocent remark.
He regards every suggestion as a personal affront,
and any criticism as a direct attack.

Lord, it's very unpleasant to live with Touchy.
     I've tried turning him out many times,
     but before I've shut the door on him
     he jumps in through the window.
     He seems to think he belongs.

I've tried reasoning with him and he says:
     'But I'm so sensitive. You don't understand.'
I've tried laughing at him
     but tears well up in his eyes and he sobs.
I've toughened him up a bit by ignoring him,
but what a relief it would be
     to get rid of him for ever.

Could you fill me with more of your spirit, Lord,
so that Touchy would be squeezed right out?

Great-aunt Maria

Great-aunt Maria is a big trial to me, Lord.
Why need she poke her long nose into everything?
Why should her shadow darken my existence?
> Breathing with every breath I draw,
> inevitably and irrevocably a part of me,
> linking me up in the chain of the generations;
> quirks, foibles, pet aversions, animosities …
All these are Great-aunt Maria flowing in my veins.

> Great-aunt Maria didn't like spiders,
> therefore I do not like spiders,
> and my daughter doesn't like spiders;
> so on, ad infinitum.

But that is quite a harmless idiosyncrasy.
There are other things, much more serious:
> tendencies,
> reactions,
> whims and fears,
> strong antipathies,
> all of them part of my built-in mechanism;
> all of them influencing my life,
> colouring my thoughts,
> and affecting my service for you, Master.

Lord, must Great-aunt Maria live with me to the
> end of my days?
Must I be me and yet her all my life through?
Can I never shake off her dominance?

Braggart

Braggart really is a pest, Master,
He makes me sick when he takes over;
boasting, boosting, embroidering.
> What he is,
> what he's done,
> what he's going to do.
Ugh! I'm disgusted with him.

Of course, I know why he does it.
Even a child has that much psychology.
He does it because he feels inferior.

But why should he feel inferior,
just because he isn't like someone else?

Lord, if Braggart would only be himself,
his very ordinary but his best self,
all would be well.

You have made us all different,
> because you want it that way, Lord.
We don't need to eat our hearts out
> because we can't sing like A,
> or write like B,
> or talk like C.

I'm always telling Braggart this,
> and basically I think he understands,
but he forgets, Master. And then he starts to brag.

Please forgive him, Lord.
He's not a bad fellow at heart,
but I find it a bit trying at times to co-exist with
        him.

The imp

In the back of my mind, Master,
       resides the imp.
Who and what he is I don't know, but he
       makes caustic comments
       on all I say or do.
In a way I suppose he keeps me in order,
for his running remarks have acted
       as a brake or a spur on many occasions.

'You a Christian!' he scorns.
'You're a fine example, I must say.
Look at the chances you have let slip today
       of showing your colours
       or saying a word for your Lord!'
But the very next day he can mutter:
'That was splendid! You really shone!
People were very much impressed …'
       and I realise
that he is tempting me to be proud.

Sometimes I wonder if he is my conscience
but I am sure he is more than that.
He is me, outside me, observing me all the time

and analysing my motives,
criticising my actions
and querying my decisions.
It is quite difficult to live with this imp
ever with me,
but I know of no way to get rid of him.
Is he for you or against you, Master?
I am never quite sure.

Niggard

What a mean old fellow Niggard is, Master!
I don't mean only with money, though that is
included,
for he was brought up to be careful
and to count his pennies.

You taught that it is better to give than to get, Lord,
but Niggard won't believe that,
or at any rate he won't practise it.
He says that what you keep you have,
and what you give away you lose.
That is why he is so mean.

But money is not his biggest weakness.
His worst fault is that he is so mean with
appreciation.
How a compliment sticks in his throat!
To ask him to say 'Well done' to another
would be to risk him choking over the words.

How can I get him to be more generous?
>To be quick to say a kindly word,
>to jump at the chance to congratulate,
>to encourage when the going is hard,
>to share another's joy.

I shall have to insist, Lord,
stand over him and say: 'Smile!'
Take him by the neck and force the issue.

I don't want this old Niggard within me, Master.
Teach me how to outwit him,
to make life so uncomfortable for him
>that he will quit for good.

In a quandary

Lord, I'm in a quandary.
>What shall I do?
Various voices rise within me and give me counsel,
>but their advice is contrary
>and I am left perplexed, bewildered.

Great-aunt Maria, old suffragette that she is,
>tells me to stand no nonsense,
>put my foot down firmly,
>let them know who they're dealing with.

Big Me sides with her.
>Those two are usually allies

when it suits their own interests.
He speaks very forcibly and even eloquently,
        pointing out the reasonableness of my
            objections.
        'You have to stand up for your rights,
        otherwise people won't respect you.
        They'll walk on you,
        using you as a doormat.'

Touchy seems very upset, but he snivels so much
        I can't understand what he's trying to say.

Then 'Saint in Embryo' breaks in.
        Quietly, persuasively,
        he argues the other side,
        and advises a peaceful, even a pleasant approach.

So what shall I do, Lord? I'm pulled in different
        directions.
I want to do what is right,
        not necessarily in other people's view.

Please, Master, show me what is best,
        and give me the courage to do it.

OTHERS

My enemy

Master, you said some hard things.
You said: 'Love your enemies.'
At first sight it does not look so difficult,
as long as I think of my enemies as out there,
      far, far away.

In jungles where matted grasses block the paths,
in hot, barren deserts where goatskin tents sprawl
      like overgrown mushrooms close to the
      baked ground,
in the cold north and southlands where they fight
      blizzards through the long, dark winters;
in great noisy cities where they drive their cars on
      the wrong side of the road.

Enemies?
They are people with features other than my own,
      neither better nor worse,
      just otherwise.
They are people with skins unlike my own,
      neither better nor worse,
      just different.
They are people with languages I can't understand,
      strange to my ears.

Those imaginary enemies that I shall never see or
      know,
      those I can think kindly of,
      those I can pray for,
      those I can love.

But, Lord, it is my enemy next door that troubles
        me.
        Her children pick my flowers,
        her dog dirties my front path,
        her drab washing flaps uglily when I have visitors;
        she is not tidy in her dress and sometimes –
        this is just between you and me, Lord
            — she smells.

Lord, do you really expect me to love *her*?
I'm quite prepared to go halfway,
        to come to some arrangement with her,
        so that we can coexist in a state of armed
            neutrality
        over the garden fence.

But *love* her?
Lord, you ask the impossible.
I can't do it.
Will you help me by showing me how to achieve
        the impossible?

About Mrs Brown

I'd like to talk to you about Mrs Brown, Lord.
To say that she and I are not on the same wavelength
        is putting it too mildly;
We are directly antagonistic and for no known
            reason.
        She is a most excellent woman.

The perfect wife mentioned in your Book couldn't
        hold a candle to her;
    yet while I admire her
    I dislike her.
    Am I simply jealous of her
    because her virtues show up my shortcomings?

I want to love Mrs Brown.
No! That's not exactly the truth, Master.
I *don't* want to love Mrs Brown!
Very definitely not.
I must put my desire in another form:
I want you to make me love her.
No! That's not true either.
I must find another formula.

I'd like you to take from me that which makes me
        dislike her.
(I'd like you to do a bit of work on her too,
        for I am sure she heartily dislikes me.)
But if you would just show me where the fault lies in me,
that would be the beginning of a new approach;
and a new approach might lead to better
        understanding,
and better understanding to mutual regard.

I'm sorry to give you all this trouble, Lord.
I ought to have brought this matter to you long ago.
        Forgive my tardiness.
In your goodness help me to get straight on this
        point,
then there will be one less problem in my life.

Someone's pet corn

Today I trod on someone's pet corn, Master,
    hard, ruthlessly but unintentionally.
How was I to know, Lord, that just that subject
     was his sore point?
    I had never seen the man before.
    Why should a few innocent remarks awake
     such anger?

I tried to think of the soft answer that might turn
    away his wrath,
but, Lord, you know I am not nimble-witted in
    such matters.
The gracious and disarming reply does not rise
    naturally and quickly within me.
So I bowed my head and let the storm pass over.

    I felt sorry afterwards, Lord,
    for he was worried,
    tense, overburdened, nervy and explosive,
    ready-laid kindling for any stray spark.
And I struck the match which made him flare.

Somewhere, there must have been a fire
    extinguisher,
    but my eyes couldn't see it,
    my hands couldn't grasp it.
    Perhaps I really didn't look for it hard
     enough . . .
     and the mischief was done.

I'm sorry, Lord.
>Sorry for that servant of yours whose nerves
>>were on edge,
>sorry that I was the stumbling-block over
>>which he tripped.
Please, dear Lord, would you bless him just now.
Let him forget this incident, as I will try to
>forget it.
Make us both just a little wiser next time we meet,
>and let us meet as friends.

A rebuke

Lord, I have received a rebuke.
>Not from you, Master,
>although I might well deserve it.
>But from a young man.
He said nothing to me;
>he did nothing to me;
>but I saw him,
>and seeing, I was humbled
>and contrite.

He sat in a restaurant, his plate before him.
>He ate like a dog, Master,
>just like a dog.
>Lapping up ice-cream with his lips and
>>tongue
>direct from the plate.

My inward reaction was swift ... and unforgivable.
    Modern youth!
    What new monstrosity will they invent?
And then I watched and understood.

His twisted arms hung uselessly on his knees.
    He was a cripple,
    a young cripple;
    going through life with a terrible defect.

And in my heart I had blamed him,
    blamed him for unseemly behaviour,
    this fine, brave lad,
    suffering people's pitying gaze
    each day of his life;
    living differently because he must;
    each day a new crucifixion.

Forgive me, Master,
I take this rebuke as from you.
Help me not to judge without knowing,
    not to jump to conclusions,
    not to condemn without evidence,
    not to hurt any of my fellow men needlessly,
    remembering that to know all is to forgive all.

A simple sum

That was a simple sum you set Peter, Master.
Seventy times seven …
Any child could give the answer:
     four hundred and ninety.
But to forgive a man four hundred and ninety times
     is a hard task;
     infinitely hard.
It goes against the grain,
like so many other of your commands.

What that person did against me was not so serious,
     but it stung my pride,
     it wounded my self-esteem.
If I've forgiven her once, I've forgiven her a dozen
     times,
     for there's the rub, Master!

It's not four hundred and ninety separate faults that I
     need your help to forgive,
I have to keep on forgiving her for the same old fault,
     way back in the past,
     done with long ago.
     I'm ashamed to own it, Lord,
     but you know it's true,
     so why should I try to hide it.

Even when I want to forgive, my forgiveness is not
     complete.
     Deep down within me a memory lies buried.

Association wakes it to life;
the reawakening brings fresh resentment;
and I have to seek your grace to forgive
again.

O Master, if you treated me like that,
where should I be?
You forgive and forget once and for all.
My sins are sunk in the bottomless sea of your
mercy and love.

Dig deep, Lord, deep into the depths of my heart,
down where these old sores lie festering.
Pour in your healing love,
teach me to forgive
as you forgive me,
once and for all.

Annabella Jones

Lord, what can I do about Annabella Jones?
How I feel about her can hardly have escaped your
notice,
for she calls out the worst in me.

At sight of her I sprout prickles all over,
feel my nerves on edge
and my temper rising.

If you ask me to define my objections, I can't do it.
      Everything about her irritates me.
      To start with, her name!

I know she isn't responsible for what her parents
      called her,
but that knowledge doesn't change my feelings
      which are quite unreasonable.
No one has the right to tack a name like Annabella
      on to plain Jones.
It isn't my business, I know, Master,
but it annoys me all the same.
What can I do about it?

Lord, I come to you,
all hot and bothered and unreasonable.
Calm me down, quieten me, make me sensible.
Teach me not to get upset over small matters.
Don't let a person's name come between us,
      nor the colour of her hair,
      nor the way she walks
      or how she talks.

Make me a better mixer with all kinds of people, Lord.
      Let me accept them for what they are,
      try to find their good points
      and overlook the rest.

People lean on me

People lean on me, Master.
>Lean heavily,
And I don't want to be leaned on.
I myself want to lean on someone else
>for support,
>for comfort,
>for understanding,
>for approval.

So what am I to do, Lord, when people lean on
>me
>for sympathy,
>for strength,
>for love,
>for prayers?

One has to be strong to be leaned on
>and I am not strong, Master,
>not in myself.
I need a new infusion of your power.

Can you so undergird and stabilise me
that I can bear up against these leanings
and offer myself as a wall of strength
>to those with trembling limbs?

Will you take away my own desire
>to lean on others,

And teach me to lean only on you, dear Lord?
 In that way I could be strong,
for your strength and courage would flow into my
  heart
  and through me out to others.
  Then when they leaned on me
  I should not fail them,
  for I should be leaning hard on you.

The hat

People get in the way, Lord,
  when I am trying to think about you in
   church;
  trying to make spiritual contact,
  to open my heart and to worship you.
Suddenly I am aware of a large hat
  right in front of my eyes,
  a large aggressive hat
  blocking my vision.
I dodge it to catch a glimpse of the altar,
I squeeze to right and lean to left
but the hat remains impenetrable.

What is even worse is that it becomes dominant in
  my thoughts.
Forgetting the altar I concentrate on the hat …
  and its wearer,
  yes, its wearer.

Who does she think she is, blocking my view like
        that?

I preen myself with a good conscience.
        My hat isn't as big as that;
        I am discreet, thoughtful of others,
        even in that detail.

Suddenly I realise what is happening.
        My intent to worship has vanished,
        my spiritual desires have cooled …
        I am hot and irritated.
In your very house I am fighting a losing battle,
        all because of a hat.
Lord, it is ridiculous that such a thing can shut you
        out
        and wake unpleasant feelings within me.

My desire to meet with you, to worship you,
        must be stronger than that.
I must see you with my inward eyes right through
        all barriers.
Help me to do just that, Master,
and also make me a little wiser where I sit next
        time.

To kick oneself

I could have kicked myself, Master!
Just after she left me I realised
    what I should have said,
    what I ought to have done
    and how I could have helped.
It was too late for second thoughts,
    for self-recrimination.
She was speeding away in her car
    her errand unfulfilled,
    her need still great,
her search still on for someone
who could help her out of a dilemma.

Was I too occupied with my own affairs
    when she called
to respond intuitively to her need?
Was my mind too slow in working,
    my heart too tepid to care,
    my link with you too frail
for you to urge me into quicker response?

This opportunity has passed into oblivion.
I am left 'kicking myself' for my failure.
Perhaps I should stop doing that and instead
ask you to make me more sensitive
    to others' problems,
and thus more able to come to their aid.

Heaven must be vast

Heaven must be a vast place, Lord!
Myriads of souls from all corners of the earth
       made welcome by your love
       for them as individuals.
It is beyond all human imagination …
Mrs Jones and Mrs Smith who attend the same
       church
       but never speak to each other
       will not easily be placed.
Their husbands, long time rivals,
are also likely to make sparks fly,
adding to the display of shooting stars.

Have you some sphere, Lord,
perhaps one of your 'black holes' in space
where such contrary characters – millions of them –
       can cool off through the ages
       until they learn more sense?

Will theological controversy cease as we pass
       the heavenly threshold,
or shall we require barriers between the sects
       to keep the peace?
Shall we challenge Peter and Paul on aspects
       of their letters in your Book,
or listen to lectures as they defend their
       standpoints?

It is hopeless, Lord, to imagine your heavenly
        realm.
        Forgive our human inability
        to comprehend your master-mind.
You will find a way to accommodate us all
in the vast Heaven prepared for your children.

TOO SMALL A SAINT

Not good enough

Master, I feel your censure over my life:
       good, but not good enough,
       warm, but not glowing,
       shallow instead of deep,
       casual instead of committed,
       indifferent instead of involved,
       soft instead of sturdy.

What can I do about it, Lord?
What is wrong?

Does self sit too securely in the saddle?
Is it body-tiredness, mental strain,
       or has it a deeper cause?
Is it the looseness of a rubber band at rest,
       or of one that has lost its stretch?
Is it the long slow decline into the valley of age?
       Passing or permanent?

You see, Lord, what a lot of questions I ask you,
and yet I don't really need any answers.
All I require is new contact with you,
       a quickening,
       a refreshing,
       a renewal.
Then I shall be able to continue.

Meet with me, Master, just now,
stretch out your hand and I will stretch out
                    mine ...
There!
Now I can go on.

Hedges

I saw it so clearly, Lord,
through the words of one of your servants.

I have built hedges around my life
            without realising it.
            Higher and higher they have grown
            without my knowledge.

These hedges have shut others out
            and myself in.
It was comfortable so, comfortable and cosy.
            Less demanded of me,
            less expected of me,
            only myself to consider.

I have hedged about my time. *My* time!
Did I create time to be my own?
Have I sovereign right to twenty-four hours a day?
Is not each hour a token of your grace?

I have hedged about my leisure.
            My free time is my own, I have said,

and I have miserly gloated over it,
resenting any encroachment upon it.

I have hedged about my love.
These, and these only, I care for,
my nearest, my dearest, my friends,
all precious because they are mine.

Forgive me, Lord. Forgive my selfish living,
my self-centredness,
my disregard of others.
Help me to tear down the high hedges I have built
and in their place to plan an open garden.
Then I can look out
and others can look in
and we shall be drawn nearer to one another.

The wheel of duty

I'm bound to the wheel of duty, Master;
It whirls round, carrying me in its dizzy turnings.
I long at times for freedom but must go on.
I say 'Stop' but it doesn't stop.
I say 'Can't' …
but I find I can because I must.

Lord, my hands hold precious things;
eternal truths are on my lips,
very often on my lips;
and I'm afraid.

Afraid of becoming mechanical.
Afraid of talking for the sake of talking,
repeating a lesson well learned.
Playing a part
with my thoughts elsewhere,
my interest elsewhere.

Don't let me become a machine, Lord,
however well adapted,
however effective,
however productive.
Help me to give myself with my message,
some of myself in everything I do:
And when pressure is heavy and the programme
packed,
come to me with some special grace.

Let me link on to your strength,
let me rest in your love,
let me remain a tool in your hands
and not become a self-propelling gadget.

Lord, I'm afraid: afraid of becoming a machine.
Only you can help me.
Come to me now.
Touch me into new awareness of your
presence;
let me remain a channel of your love,
an instrument for your use,
not a robot.

You took me too seriously

You took me too seriously, Lord.
When I said I would go anywhere for you.
I didn't mean a place like Blackpoint.
>   It's obvious that I couldn't go there.
>   You understand that, don't you?
>   The climate is damp,
>   so I might get rheumatism;
>   then the houses are built in long rows,
>   long, monotonous rows,
>   and living under those circumstances
>   might cramp my individualistic style.

I am quite willing to go anywhere for you, Master,
>   with certain reservations.
I just want this to be clear between ourselves
so that you don't ask me to do anything that is
>   beyond my normal capacity,
>   contrary to my usual custom,
>   or infringing on my personal rights.

Then when I said I would give you my all,
>   it was just a figure of speech.
>   I trust you understand it like that.
>   It was poetic language,
>   an exaggeration for the sake of making a
>   point,
>   not a statement of fact.

I know I should give and be and do all for you,
    Lord,
        but I simply haven't got that far as yet;
        perhaps one day I might.
        I know I ought to,
        but still ...
        You see ...

Tired of being unselfish

I'm tired of being unselfish, Master;
tired of taking the burnt toast,
        the cracked cup,
        the squashed tomato,
        the broken fish,
        the bruised banana,
        the smallest egg
        and so on.

It doesn't make me any less selfish either,
for I get a kick out of 'denying myself',
hearing silent applause of me by me
        in the back of my mind.

And out of the corner of my eye I see 'Saint in
        Embryo'
        fingering his halo,
        eager to don it at the slightest
        encouragement,
        thrilled to have a part to play.

So I'm tired of being unselfish, Lord,
tired of being compulsively unselfish, that is;
    urging myself from within,
    always working against the grain,
    and ever forcing the issue.

I want something better, something higher,
        something nobler,
something that only you can give me.
    I want a love for others
    that will make me want to give them the
        best;
    that their good shall be my delight
    and their joy my reward.

Is it too much to ask of you, Master,
this outgoing love that will make me forget myself,
so that I no longer think of 'denying myself'
(Self is happy to parade even under that banner)?
A positive love, not a negative restraint …
Lord, in your rich mercy will you grant me this?

Things possess me

Lord, I've made a disappointing discovery.
    Things possess me:
I'd always tried to believe that I was the ascetic
        type;
    not the real ascetic, of course,
    facts were against that,

but with tendencies in that direction.
Now I find that what is mine is very important to me,
        even if it is not of any great worth.

It must be Great-aunt Maria behind this, Lord,
for she was a miser if ever there was one.
        Bits of old string,
        paper bags,
        empty boxes and bottles …
Those were some of her more harmless
            acquisitions,
and I find that I can't throw them away without
        wincing.

I don't want to be bound by things, Lord;
        to use, yes;
        to enjoy, yes;
        to lend, sometimes;
        but to hoard,
        simply to gloat over their possession, no!

Your Book tells us a few home-truths, Master.
It reminds us that even as we brought nothing into
        this world,
so we depart, empty-handed.
It makes one think.

There must be some secret formula to follow,
        to hold in trust,
        to use wisely,
        to treasure unpossessively
        and be ready to surrender.

I have a lot to learn, Lord;
please teach me how to sit lightly to this world's
goods.

Criticism

Criticism is unpleasant, Lord.
It is bitter medicine,
administered often by a careless hand,
and it can smart and sting long after.
Why is it that all criticism seems unjustified?
Is it because we feel affronted when our
personal territory is invaded?
We are like an indignant bird,
angrily defending our garden path
with squawks and fluttering wings;
or like a wild animal circling its domain
with surly mien and warning growls.
Criticism we see as an enemy to be kept at bay.
After all, we know best!

There's the rub, Master!
We see from within, others see from without
and therefore opinions differ.
Where can the truth lie, Lord? Somewhere in
between?
Can I never be right because I see everything from
my own angle?
And are others always wrong when they see the
matter from theirs?

Master, help me not to flare up when criticised.
Help me to search for the grain of truth
        hidden in the unpalatable words,
        making up my mind to profit by it,
and to throw away the rough chaff in which it was
        embedded.
Then even my enemies will be doing me a good
        turn, Lord,
        by showing me where I can improve,
and that is something to be grateful for.

Saints

You want to make us saints, Master?
Isn't that rather a barren hope,
a pinnacle of achievement too far away in the
        clouds
        to be feasible?

Me, a saint?
With my temperament, my weaknesses, failings
        and contradictions?
You're joking, Lord!
You know the ingredients of my personality,
all I have inherited from my forebears of good and
        less good
and to be quite frank, of evil.

You set the standard too high, Lord,
and you won't leave me in peace.

You pull and push,
    nudge and prod,
You prune and discipline and train
to raise me to a higher spiritual level,
and I am like a recalcitrant donkey, kicking,
        plunging and resisting.

Why do you continue to bother with me?
Honestly, Master, the heights of holiness do call
    me,
I feel their attraction, their challenge,
    but I am way down in the valley
    and the snowy heights are distant.
Don't despair of me, Master.
Don't yield to my obstinacy and leave me alone.
Keep working at me, believing for me,
    leading me upwards.

Don't get a halo ready for me just yet,
    for it wouldn't fit.
Let me struggle and endure and aspire,
and one day I pray I may win through.

My shadow

I'm uneasy about my shadow, Lord.
    Not the shadow cast by light,
but the invisible shadow which is my influence.
Wherever I go this silent presence creeps after me,

mingles with my friends when we converse,
yet still flits around when I am silent.
It is short, touching those closest to me,
yet long, oh so long,
	stretching right into the distance,
affecting known and unknown people …
and I can't control its action.

That is a serious thought, Lord.
I can never say: 'Today I will exert a good
		influence.'
	My shadow would mock me.
	It has a life of its own,
linked and dependent on mine, it is true,
yet far freer, mobile and self-determining.

The aura of what I am pervades
		what I do and say.
It sometimes nullifies my best endeavours,
		sets at nought my well-laid plans,
		puts obstacles in my way
and shouts aloud when I command silence.

What can I do, Master,
about this shadow which is my influence on others?
Will you so dwell within me in fullness
		of your Spirit,
that my life is under your control?
Then I need not fear the effect
of my invisible shadow falling on others.

WITH CLEARER SIGHT

Make me realistic

Make me realistic, Master.
Let me define terms to myself.
I know I need a greater love for souls,
but what are 'souls', Lord?

Help me not to think of them as
       featherlight, clinic-clean wraiths
       floating invisibly around;
       interesting because unidentified,
       lovable because unknown.

Help me to remember that 'souls' are just people:
       old bodies with smelly breath and irritating
          ways,
       youngsters decked out in long hair and tight
          pants,
       children with runny noses and grimy
          fingernails,
       rich old ladies nursing lapdogs, and many
          others.

Keep me, Lord, from praying for such souls in
       general
       while ignoring my nearest neighbour.
Don't let me kid myself that I love souls
       when I can't stand the sight of Mrs Smith.
       Mrs Smith is a soul,
       doubtless a very skinny, undernourished one,

Squeezed almost out of existence by a fat, over-
nourished body,
but nevertheless a soul, a needy soul.

Make me realistic, Lord.
Open my eyes to the fact that love for souls is
simply caring about people.
It's harder put like that, Master.
Souls are comfortably distant and abstract;
people are uncomfortably near and
substantial.
It's almost a pity that I see it so clearly now,
for I'll have to do something about it.
I'll try. I really will, I promise you, Lord.

A glad spender

I want to be a glad spender, Lord,
a glad spender of my time and strength,
giving instead of withholding,
sowing instead of wanting to reap.

Don't let me be a miser, Master,
cuddling myself to myself,
careful of every effort,
counting each step,
hoarding my physical resources
for the demands of a tomorrow that might never
come.

Make me a glad spender, Lord:
  joyously giving my love and care,
  opening the sluice-gates of my small reserves,
  pouring out what little I have to give
  without measure or stint,
  without anxious debate,
  and trusting you for tomorrow.

Don't let me shelter myself in a glass case,
  fearful lest the light of day should fade me,
  dreading that the hand of time should touch me,
  shrinking from effort that might drain me,
  saving myself up … for what?
  To look nice in my coffin?

Let me give what I have to give with open hands,
offering myself to you each day for service,
happy to be used as long as life shall last,
living for you as a glad spender.
  For at the end, Lord,
  you will not ask me what I have saved,
  but what I have given.

A good programme

I had switched off,
not knowing it was coming;
so I lost a treat,
something that would have brought me joy,
moments wonderful to experience

and enriching to remember;
but I had switched off.

That happens, too, Lord, when you speak to me.
I don't always hear
because I don't always listen.
I have switched off my spiritual receiver.

And times of enrichment pass me by,
leaving me unmoved, unchanged.
I have no one to blame,
the fault is my own.
I wasn't receptive to you just then,
and my life is impoverished,
just that bit poorer,
because I wasn't listening.
I had switched off.

Help me to keep my heart open to you, Lord,
my spirit receptive,
my soul at its listening post.
For you have much to say to me,
things that I need to know,
words for my strengthening,
guidance for my way.

Keep me tuned in, Master, listening, waiting,
eager to receive;
and ready to act on
all that you have to say to me.

Those aggressive posters

It's not like in your days, Master.
The streets of Nazareth were not plastered with
　　　　advertisements.
　　Loud, aggressive posters,
　　subtle, persuasive posters –
　　　　buy this;
　　　　use that;
　　　　drink the other.

It stimulates the appetite, Lord.
　　It creates a want,
　　　　a need,
　　　　an urge,
　　to possess,
　　to be with it,
　　to live on a level with the Joneses.

Life is complex in our days, Master.
　　Shall we walk with eyes averted
　　studying the paving stones,
　　the bits of rubbish in the gutter?
Or shall we walk with upturned gaze
　　peering at the clouds chased by the wind?

What other solution is there?
　　To learn to say 'No' to these enticements?
　　But 'No' is a hard word.
　　Hard to say, but harder still to mean.

Your servant Paul said he had learnt to be content
          with what he had,
      which wasn't very much at times.
Perhaps you would help me to learn that lesson
          too,
and thus save me from falling into snares set by
          skilful salesmen.

The simple life

I'm all for the simple life, Lord.
      Just a toothbrush and towel,
      a handkerchief and comb,
      a change of clothes and shoes.

Few possessions, few demands, few worries.
What freedom of spirit when one is not cluttered
          with things!
What joy in renouncing the chains others forge for
          themselves!
What delight in simple pleasures:
      the flight of a bird,
      the scent of a rose,
      the soft patter of rain!

What are possessions but ties that bind one to
          earth,
cords that hamper the soul's free movement?
All this I know and feel, Lord.
But there is one word which upsets my equanimity.

It is a little word,
but it is powerful, Master,
and it occurs so often;
just four letters —
S–A–L–E.

What magical magnet is hidden in those letters?
The attraction of the simple life fades,
        the joys of the simple life vanish.
I am caught, impaled, tempted beyond my
                strength,
and I acquire things
        because they appear cheap,
        because they are enticingly presented,
        and skilfully advertised.
Lord, can you deliver me from sale fever?

The ant-heap

I thought of you, Lord, when I saw that ant-heap.
I stood watching it, fascinated by its ceaseless
        bustle.
        An ant-city three feet in diameter,
        an ant-world complete in itself.
Narrow paths radiated at angles into the forest,
paths tramped bare by millions of tiny ant-feet,
as great an adventure for them as our space probes.

I thought of you watching our world,
        our comings and goings,

our endless activity,
all centred on one cramped blob in space,
a small rotating orb.

What are your thoughts as you observe us?
Knowing the immensity of the universe,
do you pity us packed together so tightly
on our little ball,
hurrying, scurrying,
fretting our hearts out
if it rains on washing day
or the train is late?

O God, save us from thinking that this brief life is all.
Give us a glimpse of the vastness of eternity,
of a coming life as far exceeding this one
as that of an ant transformed to man.

When the shackles of time are broken,
when the body releases its grip on the soul,
then, then, we shall know for the first time
what it is to live,
really live.

Unfinished things

Today, Lord, I see my life like a highway,
I look back and, as far as memory can trace,
I see unfinished things thrown aside.

I have been a veritable litter-bug in this respect.
        The thrill of starting something fresh;
        the enthusiasm for a new idea;
        the joy of creating;
        then the slackening of interest as the new
            venture palled.
        Laying it aside;
        forgetting it for many days
        and finally throwing it away.

It's not wrong, Lord, to have thrown so much
            aside.
The fault was in beginning too much.
        As a child it is good to try one's skills;
        but adults must discriminate.

If I accept this, I must relinquish that;
if I give time to this, I must sacrifice that;
if I choose this, I must renounce that.

        I need wisdom, Master.
        I need your help, your guidance.
For I have only one life to live,
only so much time invested in the bank of life,
and I want my life to count.

        To count for good;
        to accomplish something useful;
        to help bring in your Kingdom.

Show me, then, what things are worthwhile, Lord,
and help me do them with all my heart and mind.

Weeds and flowers

There is one thing I should like to ask you, Lord.
     It has puzzled me often:
why do weeds grow easier than flowers?

I see it right before my eyes:
     I sow flowers and produce weeds.
     I sow grass and raise nettles;
my frail plants are choked by luscious dandelions.

Now I have no personal animosity against
     dandelions, Master.
They are bright, jolly flowers.
     Sensible too,
     for they shut up at night,
     which is more than many people do,
     judging by the noise one hears.

But why should dandelions that I don't plant
     thrive better than the flowers I protect?
How is it that from a packet of choice seeds
     I raise chickweed?

If it were only a question of flowers and weeds
     it would be strange enough,
but the tendency goes further and deeper.
     I find it within my own being,
     a downward pull,
     a gravitation to a lower level.

It is a daily fight to keep the standard high,
    to bring forth flowers instead of weeds,
    good instead of evil
    in my life, character and service.

Lord, is it a law in your moral world,
    as well as in your natural world,
that the more valuable the product
    the harder it is to produce?

Leisure

Leisure is frightening, Master:
    a string of empty hours,
    a missing day in the almanac,
    a blank page in life's book.

The stream of time slipping unnoticed through
    careless fingers;
    nothing thought,
    nothing experienced,
    nothing achieved.

A long road leading nowhere, sprouting useless
    cul-de-sacs;
    no direction,
    no purpose,
    no goal.

Help me to use leisure wisely, Lord,
    to enjoy your beautiful world,

to learn more of your marvellous creation;
to enrich my mind,
to water friendship's garden.

For one day I shall have to give account
to none other than you, Lord,
how I have used the gift of time.
Time to work, to rest, to play,
time to serve others and enjoy others.

You will ask me not only what I have done,
but what I have left undone.

Help me then not to waste one single moment.
And when no taskmaster stands over me,
when I am left to my own devices,
let me use leisure wisely,
knowing for that too
you will hold me to account.

Hidden treasure

I have a lovely secret, Master,
one that I hug closely to my heart
shared only with you and two others, both of them
gardeners.
I came upon them one dull November morning in
the park.
They were working swiftly, burying a
treasure.

With small trowels they made holes each side of
      the path
      and deep in the holes they hid hyacinth
      bulbs.
Ten minutes later when I passed the spot again
the bare brown earth stared unwinkingly at me
      as though to say: 'There's nothing here.'
But I had seen and I knew.

I hugged my delicious secret to my breast all winter
      long,
allowing myself only swift glances to right and left
      as I passed the spot.
I felt like the man in your Book, Master,
who stumbled upon treasure in a field
      and who hastily covered it over;
then with his face all innocence
he bargained and bought the field,
      knowing what lay under the rough surface.

I, too, know and wait …
My heart glows with glad anticipation every time I
      pass.
One day my treasure will appear
      and many others will share it with me
as part of your wonderful spring bounty, Lord.

O Creator God, I worship you.
Lord of life in its myriad forms and fashions,
granting us joys and satisfactions untold
in the rhythm of the yearly growth cycle,
      my heart rejoices in your power.

Sunset

I saw heaven open, Lord ...
I looked right through the clouds to the heart of being,
    the limpid glowing heart of being,
      shining through wisps of brightness.
The sense of distance was immense and
      breathcatching.
In the breaks of the serried clouds lay pale green
      islands
    fringed with red-gold haze.
In all that far-reaching stretch of glory
    I felt I belonged, Lord.
I wasn't a tiny human pigmy dwarfed by natural
      splendour,
    cowering down in fear;
I was a child of the universe, at home in that universe
    because I knew you, its Creator.

In those few moments I lived,
      enthralled, uplifted, enraptured,
    while time stood still.
All my being was suffused with radiant joy.
I was at one with you, Lord of life.
Slowly, quite slowly, the sheer bright glory faded;
    dusky shadows stole across the sky.
    The sense of awareness dulled, receded,
but I had seen and felt and I can never forget.

Master, is this a foretaste of what you have in store for us
    in the life to come?
If so, why should anyone be afraid?

LISTEN, LORD

Someone to listen

Master, the world is in a hurry,
>from morning till night,
>working, running, talking,
>busy with a thousand things.
No one has time to listen to me,
and I need to talk.

I have so much to say.
Not only small talk about everyday affairs,
>but about deeper things.
I need time to explain how I feel within me,
>the strange longings,
>the disturbing doubts,
>the questionings and probings,
>the hurts I suffer.

I don't only live on the surface, Lord.
There's a lot going on behind my quiet mien.
>Things hard to speak about,
>unless someone will listen,
>really listen to me.
>But no one has time.

So it is all bottled up within my breast,
until at times I feel that I shall burst
>with the inward pressure.

Can I talk to you, Master?
Will you listen patiently
>if my words falter at times,

if I find it hard to explain myself?
It will bring such relief if I can pour it all out to
        you,
        for you understand.
With a whole universe to govern,
you have yet time for each single soul.

Thank you, Lord!
I'm sitting at your feet now,
and you are listening,
so I begin my tale ....

Only one

Lord, you have promised to be where two or three
        meet.
That thought has been an inspiration to many.
But I am neither two nor three,
        I am only one.
        Is your promise for me too?

I remember Nicodemus coming to you at night,
        creeping stealthily up the steps
        to find you alone.
        To him you opened your heart,
        and he went out into the dark a changed
        man.

I remember the woman at the well.
        You asked her for a drink.

It was a kindly way of making contact.
And then you spoke to her,
showed what her life had been
and what it could be;
that day she would never forget.

So I take courage:
though I am alone, I do not need to feel lonely,
        to brood over the stings of life,
        to consume my own smoke
        or to bear alone a weight of sorrow.

I, too, can meet with you. I can share with you,
share my secret hopes and fears,
        talk out my distresses,
        ventilate my problems,
        and know that you understand
        and love me.

I can't pray

Your servant the apostle, Lord, told us always to
        pray,
        but I can't ...
        I simply can't.
I'm not made that way.
        My mind wanders,
        my foot twitches,
        and I remember, Lord.
Remember that I have to fetch the washing in,

that I promised to phone Mrs Farley,
that I forgot to buy flour yesterday,
and many other things.
Many, many other things.
So you understand, Master, that it is difficult for
        me to pray.

Would you mind if I just chatted to you about
        everything while it is happening?
In that way, Lord, I could keep in contact with
        you.

I could tell you of the things that worry me,
        the things that puzzle me,
        the things I detest
        and the things I enjoy.
And my longings, Master, the deep, deep longings,
        that you yourself have planted in my heart.

It may not be the highest kind of prayer,
it may not be what others can offer you,
        but it will be my way of praying,
        and I believe that you will understand
        and accept it.

Do you listen?

Do you listen, Master, when people pray?
Do you hear what they say to you?
        Every single voice that rises
        from the four corners of the earth

in infinite tongues
at all hours of the day and night,
do you listen to it all?

Did you catch the wonderful phrase in that man's
        prayer today?
        He addressed you as: 'O effulgent Majesty'.
        Do you like to be called 'effulgent Majesty'?
        Then he told you the news of the day:
        was it news to you?

Sometimes, Lord, a very sobering thought strikes me,
that you don't listen at all to what people are saying
        in their very long and wordy prayers,
        filled with well-oiled, rolling phrases,
        all of a pattern as it was in the beginning.

I'm almost afraid to follow my thought out to its
        natural sequence.
For, Master, if you don't listen to our words
        but only read our hearts and minds,
        our hidden longings and desires,
        then what we say and what we pray
        might be poles apart.
        And that thought makes me tremble.

When did I last pray to you, really pray,
my stumbling words the imperfect vehicle of my
        soul's searching,
        my silence the awe of worship in your presence?
        Lord, I have need of you just now.
        Teach me to pray,
        truly pray.

Approach

Sometimes, Lord, you come unheralded,
you enter by the side door of my heart
and are there almost before I am aware of your
        nearness.

It was so today,
there at home in the living room
as I sat with a book among children and grandchildren.
Suddenly you were there beside me,
        I knew it, I felt it,
           for my heart warmed and quickened
           to your presence,
           and a flush of joy filled me.

What unlatched the door of my heart to you, Master?
        Was it the book I was reading
        or the nearness of loved ones?
Often when I pray I don't feel you near,
but when I was not praying, you came.

Teach me the secret, Master,
of preparing a way of entrance for you
so that I can oftener feel you near,
        feel that sudden uplift of the heart,
        that stirring of the thoughts
        which heralds your approach.

I wish I knew how to keep the door open,
        forever open to your welcome intrusion.

Perhaps I am asking too much?
But thank you, Lord, that at times my blundering
        efforts succeed
in swinging open the door to allow you to pass.
May it happen more often, is my prayer.

Ill-timed prayers

It was my mistake, Lord.
I thought that event was today and found
        it took place yesterday.
There was I praying for your blessing
        on a past happening …
What do you do with such ill-timed prayers?
I cannot think, Master, that they are simply cast
        into your heavenly waste-paper basket
        as useless lumber.
Surely in the divine economy
        you will be able to use them.

Do I imagine too much when I picture
        a heavenly conveyor belt
        ceaselessly moving forward,
carrying prayers, longings, desires,
        from the past into the future?
Into that stream of directed power
        my simple prayer must have fallen;
not availing much for the particular moment
        I had in mind

but becoming a tiny drop in the strengthening
      stream of grace
      flowing before your throne
      for re-channelling earthwards.

I'm not worried then, about my mistimed prayers;
you will use them somehow, somewhere, Lord.

Let there be grass

Let there be grass in Heaven, Lord!
My awakened eyes might weary
      of the constant gleam of gold,
and long for earth's cool greening places,
its gardens, moors and meadows.

I've lived in the snowy north
      where all was whiteness,
tiring to the eyes without due protection
but pleasant to the aesthetic sense …
diamond glint of frost crystals,
gorgeous blazings of sunrise and sunset,
or purple-blue shadows lengthening on snow
          wastes.

I've lived in the torrid south
with every green blade scorched from the earth
      for the summer months.
An arid, desert landscape,
life sucked from it for a season

until rain again fell.
Hot sunshine every day can become tedious.

So I beg you, Master,
        let there be grass in Heaven!
Grass where small cherubs roll and tumble,
        tired of flying,
and where more mature angels can sit and chat,
or gently twang their harps and sing.

Please, Lord, let there be grass in Heaven,
even if I have to mow it myself.

LEARNING IN
GOD'S SCHOOL

A dunce in your school

Lord, I've muffed it again!
I'm just a dunce in your school.
>   I knew I had failed,
>   and you knew it too,
>   but you said nothing.
Have patience with me!
I'm always going over the same old lessons
and never really learning them.

I was so sure I could handle that situation.
>   I've had plenty of experience of it
>   and through trial and error have learnt what
>   not to do,
>   so I had the theory all right.

I'm sure that if you tested me in theory only
>   I could make a better showing.
>   But you are not satisfied with theory.
>   You insist upon practice,
>   and that is where I fail.

Why, Lord, should there be such a gulf fixed
>   between theory and practice?
>   To know what to do
>   and yet not do it;
>   to see the pitfalls
>   and yet stumble into them?

Do you tire of having such a poor pupil
and feel like washing your hands of me?

Give me another chance!
Perhaps you can show me a better way to learn my
        lessons,
        so that I don't fail so often.
I want to learn, I really do.
I'm beginning to see that the secret is
        to keep in close touch with you,
        rather than to rely on theoretical knowledge
        or my own endeavours.

Teach me then, Master, so that I can make some
        progress;
I don't want to stay for ever as the dunce in your
        school.

A mixed bunch

What made you decide on your twelve disciples,
        Master?
They were a rather mixed bunch when you took
        them in hand,
if you don't mind my saying so.
        Hot-tempered zealots,
        ambitious place-seekers,
        rough-worded fishermen,
        and just ordinary folk.
But they turned out well, all but one,
        and that was not your fault
        for you tried to save him.

When I look around at your followers of today,
we, too, seem rather a mixed bunch.
Some stand out like giants among their fellows,
but the rest of us are very ordinary.
You seem to have a flair for picking out unlikely
individuals
and finding a use for them.

Why, Lord, did you call me to follow you?
What a lot of trouble you would have saved
yourself
if you'd let me go my own way.
Did you really want me in your following
or were you trying to save me from myself?

Thank you a thousand times for that beckoning
finger
and the impulse you gave me to respond.
I wish I'd been more loyal to your
leadership,
profited more from your teaching
and been a better representative of yours.

But I do thank you, for you filled my life with
meaning;
you gave me a settled purpose,
broadened and deepened my thinking,
and helped me to meet life's storms with a steady
keel.
So thank you, Master.
From the depths of my heart, thank you.

Kind to the unthankful

Lord, your Book says that you are kind to the
        unthankful.
      I'm not like that, Master.
      I'm kind until people prove unthankful,
      and then I feel like leaving them to it,
      washing my hands of them.

But you go on being kind,
      even against anger and hate,
      scorn and cold indifference,
      wooing with love the hardened hearts of
        men.

Why do you do it, Lord?
Do you spy the glint of gold among the rubble?
Can you see the makings of a man in a ne'er-do-
      well?
Or sense the texture of fine womanhood in a slut?
Or can you do it just because you are you?
      Because you really do care about people,
      really love them in spite of their nastiness?

I think that must be the secret,
      and that is why I react so differently.
You pour out love in such abundance
      that it sweeps around and over all obstacles.
You love because it is your nature to love
      without thought of recompense or return.

Is love like that something one can learn,
          Master?
          Or has it to be a gift,
          a gift from you?
          If so, will you grant it me
          in the measure that I can contain it?

A distorted picture

You must forgive us, Master.
We mean well when we talk so much of your love
          and soft-pedal your anger;
but we are giving a distorted picture,
          a wrong image,
          a one-sided view of you.

We avoid the issue by omitting to read
          your scornful words on subterfuge,
          your hatred of hypocrisy,
          your blazing anger against injustices,
          your sharp words to tricksters.

You lashed out against the religious humbugs of
               your day;
          'play actors' you called them,
          'hypocrites' you hurled at them,
          'blind leaders of the blind',
          'brood of vipers' …
          You did not spare hard words.

You couldn't expect to be popular when you used
        such language.
        You cut across vested interests,
        you stirred up hatred,
        you created enemies,
        and you paid the penalty with your life.
Help us, Lord, to remember your anger against
        deceit.
        Don't let us imagine we can double-cross
        you,
        pretending to be what we are not,
        or think that we can sow without reaping.

Lord, you are flaming justice as well as tender love;
give us a wholesome fear of your condemnation.

Incredible!

It's incredible, Master,
beyond all understanding
that you should be willing to identify yourself with
        the human race.
What is there to commend us?
You know the whole long story of our vicious
        passions,
so I don't need to elaborate;
and you chose to become one with us,
to be born of lowly parentage in a cattle shed.
        Incredible!

It might be argued that you didn't know just how
             bad we were before you came,
             but you certainly soon found out.
Yet your favourite name for yourself was Son of
             Man.
Weren't you ashamed openly to link yourself with
             humans,
             knowing us as we are?
Yet you did it, and did it willingly.

Sometimes I get a glimpse of what it must have
             cost you,
             this humiliation,
             this self-imposed limitation,
             coming down to our level –
you, the source of all life, limited in movement and
             power;
you, immortal and eternal, binding yourself with
             the chains of time;
you, the mighty ocean, willing to live as a single
             droplet;
you, Lord of all, becoming a village carpenter;
you, the sinless one, dying for our sins.
             Incredible, yet true!

Thank you, Lord, because you did it –
             for my sake,
             for all of us.
             Thank you!

This fellow

You had many taunts flung at you, Master,
        as you trod this earth of ours.
Insults, scorn and hatred flourished round you,
        but perhaps the most barbed of all
        were the contemptuous words:
'This fellow welcomes bad people and eats with
        them.'

It was intended as a smack in the face for you,
        Lord.
        You went to parties and weddings,
        as well as to sick-beds and funerals.
        At one time you were quite popular
        and even sought after,
but you were not very discriminating
        in the type of folk you mixed with,
        so they thought you didn't know.

Didn't know that rich clothing hid a grasping,
        selfish heart,
that flowing robes concealed a harlot's body;
that compliments were but the grappling irons of a
        trap,
        a trap to catch you,
        and kill you.

As though you didn't know …
You with the steady eyes that saw through people,
with the keen perception that weighed motives
and quickly summed up character.

You gave them an answer:
what was meant as a gibe, you took as a compliment.
    You put your cards on the table
    and told them straight out:
'I'm not looking for good people, but for bad.'
They hated you all the more for that remark,
    for it baffled them.

But it gives us courage to come to you. Master.
We know that you welcome such as we are.
You welcome crooked characters to put them
        straight,
you welcome the sick at heart to make them well,
you welcome sinners to make them saints.
You welcome me. For that I thank you.

Step by step

Walking is a funny business, Master,
    and so very personal.
One step after another, each step counting,
and each taking one nearer to or further from the
        goal.

The spiritual walk is also step by step
    by one's own effort.
When you first challenge, Lord,
    the initial response seems exciting,

101

a tremendous forward surge into the
unknown,
then the pace appears to slacken as the
pilgrimage lengthens.

But it is still step by step.
There is no hiking in the spiritual life,
no thumbing a lift with Peter or Paul,
no chartering a denominational coach
or booking a seat
in an ecclesiastical jumbo jet bound for Paradise.

It would be a lonely business,
walking the spiritual pathway,
if it were not for your companionship, Lord.
It's such prosaic plodding at times,
left foot, right foot, without end,
the first enthusiasm abating while the goal's still
out of sight.

Keep me going, Lord,
keep me persevering,
though at times footsore, blistered, weary.
Thousands of other pilgrims are on their way
to your heavenly city.
Let me greet them cheerily,
taking courage from their steadfastness,
and may my direction be right,
even if my pace is slow.

No secrets

There can be no secrets between you and me,
>Master,
>>and I am glad about that,
I can carry off a camouflage with other people.
A sudden shopping emergency sees me sally forth,
a neat coat hiding my worn overall
with its newly acquired spots of paints
>>(I do slosh it around rather generously).
I wouldn't like Mrs Black to know what my coat
>hides,
for she would gloat for ages over my slovenliness.

Then I can control my impatience with certain
>people up to a point,
>>for rather a limited space of time, I admit.
I kid myself that I am getting through nicely
but you know quite well how I am boiling inside.
You see the rising resentment that my time is being
>abused,
>>the growing irritation
while my face still wears – at least I hope it does –
>a sympathetic smile.
You hold your peace but I seem to catch
>a reproachful look.

Lord, I can't wear my heart on my sleeve.
I must hide some of my feelings from curious
>gazes.
Sometimes I have to suppress a bitter
>disappointment,

trying not to reveal how wounded I am.
It is such a relief then, Master, to realise that you
know all,
With you I don't need to act a part,
pretending to appear other than I am,
and for that I am very grateful, Lord.

Martyrdom

Martyrdom has its pain, Master,
but it also has its pleasure;
the subtle satisfaction of nursing a grudge,
gloating over it,
magnifying it,
building it up from a brick to a high-rise tower
where it dwarfs all near it.
That pleasure, that sneaky selfish pleasure, I have
known.

It is nothing to boast about, Lord,
this ability to wear the martyr's crown at the
slightest opportunity,
noting with dulcet joy the regret on others' faces,
hearing the concern in their voices,
while all the time one wears a patient, resigned air.

True martyrdom has none of those delicate
delights;
one person suffers while the rest gloat;
but in false martyrdom all around suffer
while one revels in self-pity, in breast-hugging
abasement

and in stealing the limelight, however sickly
        its beam.

Lord, the true martyr's crown is not for me,
but in your mercy, in your boundless mercy,
        save me from the false kind.
Save me in spite of myself and my baser leanings,
pull me up with a start when I begin to think
        myself badly done by,
        overlooked, overworked or unappreciated,
when little devils of temper whisper in my ears:
        'It's a shame how they treat you!'

Master, teach me to speak out at such moments,
not hotly but rationally, if I feel I am put upon.
Deliver me from smouldering resentment which
        can burst into a blaze
        enveloping me with flames
        and creating a spurious martyr's stake on
        which I burn,
        consumed from within myself.

Towards you, Lord

I saw them this morning, Master,
        tightly clenched praying hands,
lifted in mute worship to a Creator-God.
They were only the newborn leaves of a row of
        seedlings
        still wrinkled and twisted;

but their fervent stretching into the unknown
upper world
touched me deeply.

They were obeying an inner urge, bewildered yet
joyful,
after having pierced through earth's crust:
reaching timorously but strongly upward not
knowing how far they must go
before nature said enough.
Not knowing the storms of rain and wind they
would meet,
the attacks of enemies unknown;
disobeying the law of gravity to fulfil their destiny
by obeying the higher law of growth.
Hearing nature's call to rise out of seeming death
to pulsing life, rising sap,
growth and expansion;
to the final revelation of the hidden bud and seed.

So may I, Lord, respond to that call from you
which disturbs my heart,
making me dissatisfied with earthly things,
with finite aims,
and filling me with longings inexpressible
for something beyond,
something to which you challenge me.
Grant me the pluck to do as the seedlings did,
to dare to answer,
confident, believing,
to stretch my hands upwards, towards you, Lord.

UNKNOWN TOMORROWS

Time

What has happened to time, Master?
The clock ticks on as usual
> but the measure of its hours seems erratic.
When I was young there was a vast expanse of time
> between sunrise and sunset,
> enough to live a whole life in,
> each moment crammed with activity.
Now a day slips by unobtrusively
> without leaving any trace of its passing.
> It is here, then gone.

As a child I thought eternity stretched
> from one Christmas to the next,
the monotony of slowly passing months
> only broken by a brief summer holiday.
Now I hardly put the seasonal decorations away
> before it is time to unbox them again.

Time appears to be elastic, Lord,
stretching or contracting in a disconcerting way.
The waiting for a telephone call or a letter
> is time spun out to its thinnest thread
> and longest dimension
but hours of joyous fellowship flit hastily by,
> compacted into utter brevity.

This teaches me one thing, Master …
not to reckon life by passing days
> but by true living.

One single hour can contain more of value than a
           year.
Help me, Lord, to remain vital and responsive,
           interested and involved,
receiving the precious hours as a gift from you
           to be enjoyed as they slip away.

Growing old with grace

Help me to grow old with grace, Lord!
Even as I pray the words I smile to myself,
for grace, physical grace, is somewhat lacking
           from my stiff joints and slow movements.
Gone is the limber lightness of youth,
the rapid action and supple swiftness,
each muscle part of a well-trained whole.
           The years have taken their toll,
and that kind of grace is beyond me now.

It is inward grace I crave, Master,
           the grace of gratitude for the past.
I call up the good moments, the joyous memories;
I relive happy scenes and savour brief triumphs.
It's been a long life but a good life.
For all this and much more, I thank you.

Then I ask, Lord, for the grace of humour.
Help me still to see the funny side of living,
           to enjoy a joke,
           and even make one myself!

To laugh when I fumble in my purse for coins
        or when memory slips a cog.

Finally, I ask for the grace of patience:
to await with hope, to endure to the end.
Not to lose out on the last lap of the race
        because of flagging spirits.
Jerk me into a lively interest in my surroundings,
        in the world events of the day.
Don't let me settle into a snug cocoon of self-
                interest.
        Keep me alive and alert in mind,
even when the body no longer responds with
                alacrity.
Lord, help me to grow old with grace.

A human caterpillar

I'm just a caterpillar, Master,
        earthbound and clumsy,
        heavy feet hugging the ground;
        a crawler,
        eyes glued to a cabbage leaf.
        Slow, painfully slow in progress.
Limited activity, limited vision, limited horizon.

But, in my heart, my caterpillar-heart, I dream …
dream of the day when I shall shed my cumbrous
                clothing,
        say goodbye to my clodfootedness,

rise from my chrysalis-coffin
and on flashing wings skim the eternities of the
          upper sphere.

          Free! Free at last,
          free of my former fetters,
          denizen of another world.
'This perishable thing clothed with the imperishable,
this mortal clothed with immortality.'
          O great, glad day!
          O hope within my soul,
          O glorious promise,
          destiny divine!

But just now, Lord, I'm still at the crawling stage,
          earthbound and clumsy,
          heavy feet hugging the ground,
          slow, painfully slow in progress.

In your goodness grant me this favour, dear Lord;
let not my sluggish gait rob me of my vision.
          I shall rise
          clothed with immortality
          to join you in the Great Beyond!
It is your own promise, Lord, and on that promise
          I rely.

Poor old soul

I used to say that myself, Master,
when in my bumptious youth I thought
        that anyone over thirty was finished, *out* ...
and that at forty, one had a foot in the grave;
yet here I am at the three-score-year-and-ten mark,
        still apparently going strong
        and quite happy to be old.

I wouldn't want to live my life over again, Lord.
There have been too many painful passages,
        too many struggles,
        too many disappointments ...
I feel like a ship that is entering a long-sought
        harbour,
        storm-worn, with sun-blistered paint
        yet chugging along on the old faithful
        engine
        towards a final docking.

Youngsters now think of me as a 'poor old soul'!
They can save their pity for I need none.
        I like being old,
        I enjoy being old.
The questings and questionings are mostly behind
        me;
my expectations are modest so there are less
        disillusions,
        my wants are not many,
        my needs even fewer.

In your goodness you have granted me a kind of
          wisdom
so that my reaction to unpleasant news is not as
          violent,
          my judgments not so harsh.
This mellowing is one of the bonuses of growing old
          for which I thank you, Lord.

So this 'poor old soul' is a happy and fulfilled old
          soul.
          Thank you, Master, for your great part in
          that.
With you I can make the last bit of the way.

Dangling leaves

I saw them in the park this morning, Lord,
          and I chuckled to myself,
for I'm just like them.
Other leaves had withered and fallen
          obeying nature's mysterious laws
but a few individualists remained dangling on the
          branches,
weathered pennants of a season's storms.
          Withered, yes,
          their rich colours fading,
          but still alive
          and – if leaves can kick – kicking.

They were enjoying themselves dancing in the
          autumnal gusts

and my heart danced with them.
They exulted in the strong wind, even mocked it,
      I felt,
      for they still hung on,
      grimly but triumphantly.
My season is over too, Lord, but *I* hang on
with sufficient strength and humour to make it
      worthwhile.
      The sap of life still flows in my veins,
      enough to withstand life's tempests.
Though wrinkled and faded, I'm still game.

One day some harsh frost or boisterous wind
      will get the better of me.
My tenuous hold on life will snap
      and my body will return to the soil where it
      belongs,
      yielding itself willingly to Mother Earth
      while my spirit returns to you.
Until then, Master, keep my courage high.
Let me play the game right to the finish
      then not quarrel when the end comes.
It's been a good life, Master, with your aid.

Death but a door

Master, I thank you,
for you have removed a black cloud from my
      horizon
      by taking from me the fear of death.
I have come to realise that death is but a door,

a door into the larger, fuller life of the spirit.
Through that door we all have to pass.
>   One day it will be my turn
>   but I am not afraid.

What awaits me on the other side?
>   I wish I knew more ...
It is a strange thought that I shall embark on that
>   last journey
>   with no ticket, no luggage and no money,
I who have always made such careful preparations
>   for every little trip.
This time there will be just me ... and you.

I can never think of Heaven as 'up there'
>   for it's around us now,
>   in another dimension closed to our earthly
>   senses.
In escaping from the body we qualify to enter
>   the realm of the spirit.
It will be a fantastic adventure,
>   like a baby thrust from the womb to the
>   world.

Don't let my loved ones sorrow for me when I go, Lord.
Let them think of me emerging into more
>   abundant life
>   with much greater fulfilment
>   and added joys.
Let them remember that I shall still be in your hands,
>   still the object of your love and care,
and let their hearts be comforted.

Sitting lightly to life

Help me, Lord, to sit lightly to life,
to be ready to rise from my place
      when the summons comes to meet you,
      empty-handed and alone.

Let my grasp loosen on my few possessions.
Don't let me try to lug them with me, Lord,
      clambering up the heavenly staircase
      clutching my dainty fruit knives
      and some favourite books
      and trailing my tape recorder.
Other spheres will have other treasures,
so let me go in glad anticipation of what awaits me.

Let me leave my garden to another's care,
glad for the days when I could tend it,
      grateful for colour and fragrance,
      not grudging the hours of toil it entailed
but considering them an investment for someone
      else's pleasure.

My home I thank you for, Master,
      I have needed its shelter.
During years it has been a comfortable shell
      round my vulnerable body
      but now I must leave it.
Let me throw a glance of recognition around,
      grateful for all memories.

Let me wave a plucky farewell to my dear ones,
>   those who are left
>   for most have gone before,
knowing that I shall meet them again in your
>   presence.

So I sit lightly to life, Master,
>   awaiting your summons
>   whenever you send for me.

A flickering candle

A flickering candle is no pleasant sight.
Had it tongue to speak, what might it say?

Look not on what I am now,
>   but what I was.
>   Tall, straight, shapely.
Bravely I shed my light on all around,
knowing that as I gave, I was myself consumed.

Harsh winds of life beat upon me,
>   challenging my right to shine,
>   fluttering my flame hither and thither.
>   My strength dripped from me,
>   yet I remained alight,
>   faintly flickering.

Lord, this flickering candle speaks to me.
I, too, have known the pride of youth and strength,
held my head high and daily done my tasks.

But now the sun has passed its zenith,
strain and stress of duties have taken their toll,
winds of change have whirled around me,
      but by your grace,
      my light still burns.

Grant me one favour, Master.
Let my light flicker until the end,
until my flame sinks spent
      into final rest.

Tomorrow

Tomorrow is an X-day, Lord,
an unknown quantity of unknown quality.
I'm not even sure that there will be a tomorrow.
      It's a might-be, not a shall-be.
So far in my life sunrise has always followed sunset,
      but it won't always be so.

What does tomorrow conceal in its travelling bag?
      Joyous surprises?
      Let them all come.
      Good news?
      I'm thirsting for it.

Or there might possibly be sorrows …
      the death of a loved one?
If so, help me to be grateful for the hours we
      shared,

let memories bind a golden chain.
Is sickness in the offing?
Let me learn lessons of patience and endurance.

Catastrophe may suddenly strike me:
      road accident?
      train crash?
      air disaster?
      who knows?

Life has many ingredients, some good, some bad.
All kinds must come my way at some time.

Keep my heart steady, Lord, whatever tomorrow
      may bring.
Let me hold your hand and walk unafraid with
      you;
for finally, Master, you will write one word
      over my earthly life,
      and that word will be
      FINIS.

SOURCES

All the prayer poems are drawn from *Just a Moment, Lord* (Hodder and Stoughton 1973), except for the following:

> From *Between You and Me, Lord*
> (Hodder and Stoughton 1975)
> The hat, Hidden treasure, Sunset, Approach, Step by step, No secrets, Martyrdom, Time, Poor old soul, Dangling leaves, Death but a door, Sitting lightly to life.

> From *Towards You, Lord*
> (Hodder and Stoughton 1978)
> Courage for today, This one day, Criticism, Saints, My shadow, Towards you, Lord; Growing old with grace.

> From *God in my Everyday*
> (Hodder and Stoughton 1984)
> Tides, Heaven must be vast, Ill-timed prayers, Let there be grass.

> From *My God and I* (SP&S Ltd 1993)
> The imp, To kick oneself.

A comprehensive collection of Flora Larsson's prayer poems and other writings, *Just a Year, Lord,* arranged as a book of daily readings for a year, was published by the United Kingdom Territory in 2001.

An earlier selection from her writings, *From my Treasure Chest*, was published by SP&S Ltd in 1981.

Flora Larsson is also the author of *My Best Men are Women* (Hodder and Stoughton 1974) and five short biographies of Salvation Army personalities.

Can be purchased from any Salvation Army trade or supplies department and online at www.amazon.co.uk

Essentials of Christian Experience
Classic Salvationist Text
Frederick Coutts

Originally published in 1969, this book permits the 21st century reader an insight into the thoughts which General Coutts shared with many thousands of people in a variety of locations and situations during the time of his ministry.

128pp (paperback)
ISBN 978-0-85412-838-9

Other titles in the *Classic Salvationist Texts* series include:
Purity of Heart – William Booth
Practical Religion – Catherine Booth
The Desert Road to Glory – Clarence Wiseman
The Common People's Gospel – Gunpei Yamamoro
What and Why we Believe – Harry Dean
An Adventure Shared - Catherine Baird

A Pilgrim's Song

the autobiography of
Jarl Wahlström

The English language
edition of the
autobiography of Jarl
Wahlström – the
twelfth General of The
Salvation Army and
the first Finnish
officer to be elected
to that role. In this
book, first published
in Finnish in 1989,
the author describes how,
as one of God's pilgrims, he was uniquely
privileged to witness the work of The Salvation
Army in some of the remotest parts of the world.
Jarl Wahlström served as General from 1981 to
1986, and throughout these pages the reader will
sense how he thanks God for his pilgrimage and
the hope of an eternal goal.

192pp (paperback), 41 photographs
ISBN 978-0-85412-845-7

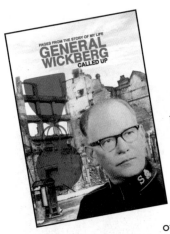

Called Up – Pages from the Story of my Life

the autobiography
of Erik Wickberg

The English
language edition of
the autobiography
of Erik Wickberg – the
ninth General of The Salvation Army and a
testimony to the rich life to be found in the
service of God. This book, first published in
Swedish in 1978, describes how, having spent his
formative years in Sweden, Germany and
Switzerland, Erik Wickberg then served as a
Salvation Army officer in those countries as well as
the United Kingdom. His vast knowledge of
languages and thorough appreciation of different
cultures stood him in good stead when he was
elected to the office of General in 1969. Serving as
the Army's international leader for the next five
years, he oversaw and visited many aspects of the
Army's ministry on every continent. This book
provides a moving and colourful account of his life,
including fascinating insights into his role as liaison
officer in Sweden during the years of the Second
World War.

168pp (paperback), 13 photographs
ISBN 978-0-85412-846-4

Called To Preach – Sermons by Salvationist Women

A collection of 35
sermons penned
by women Salvation
Army officers from
around the world and
including *The Times*
2000 'Preacher of the
Year' award-winning 'The
People Who Walked in
Darkness Have Seen a
Great Light', by Colonel

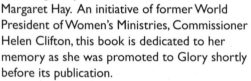

Margaret Hay. An initiative of former World
President of Women's Ministries, Commissioner
Helen Clifton, this book is dedicated to her
memory as she was promoted to Glory shortly
before its publication.

208pp (paperback)
ISBN 978-0-85412-839-6